Remembering
Washington, D.C.

Matthew Gilmore and Andrew Brodie Smith

TURNER
PUBLISHING COMPANY

The first separate building to house the Library of Congress, the Jefferson Building opened to the public in 1897. Architects Smithmeyer and Pelz based the front facade partly on the Paris Opera House. The library was the first fully expressed Beaux-Arts building in Washington, and more than 40 painters and sculptors were involved in the building's decoration.

Remembering
Washington, D.C.

Turner Publishing Company
4507 Charlotte Avenue • Suite 100
Nashville, Tennessee 37209
(615) 255-2665

Remembering Washington, D.C.

www.turnerpublishing.com

Library of Congress Control Number: 2010924248

ISBN: 978-1-59652-638-9

Printed in the United States of America

ISBN: 978-1-68336-903-5 (pbk)

10 11 12 13 14 15 16—0 9 8 7 6 5 4 3 2 1

Contents

This image depicts the cash vault inside the Department of Treasury after 1910.

ACKNOWLEDGMENTS

This volume, *Remembering Washington, D.C.,* is the result of the cooperation and efforts of a number of organizations and individuals.

We would like to thank in particular the Library of Congress and the Washingtoniana Division of the D.C. Public Library.

We would also like to thank staff at the Washingtoniana Division and the Washington Star Collection for their assistance:
Mark Greek, Ryan Semmes, Faye Haskins, Jason Moore, Michelle Casto, and the chief of the division, Karen Blackman-Mills. Don Hawkins and Michael Harrison also provided useful insights.

—Matthew Gilmore and Andrew Brodie Smith

PREFACE

Washington, D.C., has hundreds of thousands of historic photographs, scattered through thousands of institutions across the United States. Many are widely published. This book brings together more than 100 images from the collections of the Library of Congress and the Washingtoniana Division of the D.C. Public Library.

The photographs chosen for inclusion here suggest the richness of the collections from which they came. The Library of Congress images include those of numerous acclaimed photographers, including Frances Benjamin Johnston, Lewis Hine, and Gordon Parks, as well as lesser known photographers of the Farm Security Administration–Office of War Information, like Esther Bubley, Martha Roberts, David Myers, and John Vachon. The Washingtoniana photographs include those from the collections of Hugh Miller and Joseph Curtis.

The book is divided into four sections. The first section covers the Civil War era. The second section spans the 1880s to the 1920s. Section 3 moves from the 1920s to 1949. Section 4 concludes the book covering the 1950s to 1963.

Each section contains photographs illustrating the life and fabric of Washington, particularly that of a vanished downtown Washington. One can see the slow changes in (or remarkable persistence of) the architecture of Pennsylvania Avenue. Similarly, change came slowly to F and 7th streets. Much more dynamic is the street life—pedestrians, horses, wagons, streetcars, automobiles, and buses. We can measure the passage of time as these things change. In addition to hometown Washington, we see the evolution of the city of political theater, from the Grand Army Review and its diminishing echoes—the Grand Army of the Republic encampments, the presidential inaugural parades, and other marches on Pennsylvania Avenue—until groups swelled far beyond the capacity of that space and took to the Mall.

We illustrate a city under threat in the Civil War to a city of threatened promise in the 1960s, through its downtown, citizens, and monumental works.

The goal in publishing this work is to provide broader access to a set of extraordinary photographs. The aim is to inspire, provide perspective, and evoke insight that might assist officials and citizens, who together are responsible for determining Washington's future. In addition, the book seeks to preserve the past with respect and reverence.

With the exception of touching up imperfections that have accrued with the passage of time and cropping where necessary, no changes have been made. The focus and clarity of many images are limited to the technology and the ability of the photographer at the time they were recorded.

We encourage readers to reflect as they explore Washington, D.C., stroll along its streets, or wander its neighborhoods. It is the publisher's hope that in making use of this work, longtime residents will learn something new and that new residents will gain a perspective on where Washington has been, so that each can contribute to its future.

—*Todd Bottorff, Publisher*

The Supreme Court building, inspired in part by the design of Roman temples, was completed in 1935. The design belonged to renowned New York architect Cass Gilbert, who puts his likeness on the pediment over the central entrance. The building is made of a brilliant white Vermont marble.

To the End of the Civil War Era
(1860–1879)

In what amounted to a great psychological victory for Union forces, architect of the Capitol Thomas U. Walter designed and oversaw the construction of a stunning new dome for the Capitol during the Civil War. This photo captures the construction as of the time of Lincoln's first inauguration in 1861.

2

The General Post Office building at the corner of 8th Street and E Street, N.W., was designed by architects Robert Mills (the Washington Monument) and Thomas U. Walter (the U.S. Capitol dome). It was the first marble building in Washington and housed the nation's first public telegraph office. It served as a hospital during the Civil War and housed General Pershing's office at the close of World War I.

Montgomery Meigs designed the Pennsylvania Avenue bridge over Rock Creek, constructed between 1857 and 1862. As a part of the Washington Aqueduct, the iron pipes carried the city's water supply. Too narrow for its traffic load from the start, it was replaced with a new bridge, constructed around the cast-iron pipes and completed in 1916.

This famous view, taken from the top floor of the General Post Office, shows the original south wing of the Patent Office and some of the surrounding wood and brick domestic architecture characteristic of early Washington city (ca. 1846).

In 1861 there were 800 iron and 30 brass cannons at the Arsenal (some of which are visible here). The arsenal was located at Greenleaf Point, at the junction of the Potomac and Anacostia rivers, and was joined in 1829 by the penitentiary designed by Charles Bulfinch. The complex was later named Fort Humphries (and now Fort McNair).

An 1860s view of the Chesapeake and Ohio Canal, the Potomac, and the Aqueduct Bridge to Alexandria, taken from a spot below Georgetown University. Neither the C&O Canal nor the (short-lived) Alexandria Canal were an economic success for Washington, the Alexandria Canal closing in 1886 and the C&O in 1923. Georgetown became an economic backwater as its harbor silted up and the canals failed.

The Sanitary Commission (founded by citizens including Henry Whitney Bellows and Dorothea Dix) was a civilian agency that supplemented the medical corps during the Civil War. It was staffed by some of the finest physicians in the country. This image depicts the staff of a local Sanitary Commission "lodge"—a unit of the Commission, usually located near a railroad station, that provided temporary shelter for wounded and sick soldiers. Sanctioned in 1861, the Commission was disbanded in 1866.

In 1847, at the age of 29, architect and engineer James Renwick, Jr., designed the Smithsonian Institution Castle. The building, made of red Seneca sandstone, is considered an excellent example of medieval revivalism. This picture was taken before a devastating fire in January 1865, caused by an improperly installed stove pipe, which damaged the building and destroyed collections.

Long Bridge, seen here in a Civil War–era photograph, was reconstructed in 1835. It served both rail and regular traffic and linked Washington, D.C., to its Southern battlefields. Photographer Andrew Joseph Russell (1830–1902) was a photographer-engineer for the United States Military Railroad Construction Corps. The sign at the top of the bridge says, "Walk your horses."

Despite the pressures of war, the grounds of the Arsenal still attracted those seeking leisure. A typical group is shown here in front of the headquarters (ca. 1862). The arsenal in Washington would later be the site of the execution of Lincoln's assassins.

The Aqueduct Bridge, which was formed from a large wooden trough supported by eight solid-masonry piers (an engineering marvel in its day) was built to connect the C&O and Alexandria canals. It would be planked over for use as a bridge during the Civil War. Restored to private ownership in 1866, in 1923 it was replaced with Key Bridge.

Called the Old Capitol Prison because the building was built to serve temporarily as the seat of Congress after the British burned the Capitol in 1814, the prison housed some of the most prominent Confederate spies and generals during the Civil War. The U.S. Supreme Court building now stands in the general location once occupied by the prison.

The Washington Aqueduct was one of the finest examples of civil engineering design in the United States before the Civil War, stretching from Great Falls to Washington, D.C. Water first flowed through it in 1863 and it has been in continuous service since. This bridge, Bridge No. 3, is the Griffith Park Bridge, over Mountain Spring Branch. Two hundred feet long and built of masonry, it has a 75-foot arch. The ghostly outlines of a man and horse are just visible beneath the arch, telltale evidence of the technological limits of early photography.

Mason's Island (originally Analostan Island) belonged to the Mason family. During the Civil War it was occupied by the Union Army. Camp Greene on the island was the training ground for black troops, which formed the First Regiment United States Colored Troops (USCT). Abandoned after the Civil War, the island was purchased in 1931 and renamed Theodore Roosevelt Island. The Roosevelt Memorial was dedicated there in 1967.

This 1863 view of the Capitol building shows Thomas U. Walter's new dome nearly completed. Walter chose a cast-iron dome rather than a traditional masonry one because it was cheaper and lighter and could be erected more quickly.

Georgetown, founded in 1752, preceded the foundation of the City of Washington and remained a separate municipality until after the Civil War. The Forrest-Marbury House is the large house to the left. It was here, at a dinner hosted on March 29, 1791, by Revolutionary War hero Gen. Uriah Forrest, that the agreement was reached to secure the land along the Potomac River that would become the District of Columbia. This view, from the western end of Georgetown, shows the main thoroughfare Bridge Street (now M Street) and the clusters of various buildings clinging to the slope from street to canal to river.

President Andrew Jackson chose architect Robert Mills' design for the Treasury Building in 1836. The building was constructed over nearly four decades, during which time other architects, including Thomas U. Walter, made substantial changes to Mills' original plan. The south entrance to the building, depicted here during the Civil War, looks much as it does today.

The cities of Washington and Georgetown were ringed with forts and camps, including this one on the highlands at Tennallytown (now Tenleytown), here at the intersection of what is now River Road and Wisconsin Avenue. Fort Reno in the distance is the highest point in the District. The 55th New York Infantry served in the defenses of Washington from 1862 to 1865. Colonel Baron DeTrobriand recruited this regiment of infantry, consisting chiefly of Frenchmen, mainly from New York City.

The 1848 Winder Building served as the headquarters for the Signal Corps. In 1865, the Signal Corps used flags to communicate to military camps around the city from the roof of the Winder Building. "Sic transit gloria mundi" (thus passes the glory of the world) was the final transmission to the Army of the Potomac in 1865.

This is another image of the Sanitary Commission "lodge" near C St., N.W., in Washington. Wounded soldiers were temporarily cared for here. The Sanitary Commission was a civilian agency that supplemented the medical corps during the Civil War.

An 1865 view from above Georgetown. Georgetown (George Town originally) comprised only a few blocks along the Potomac when founded. Some great estates, such as Tudor Place, occupied the hills above. The town slowly expanded into the hills above, along the spine of High Street (Wisconsin Avenue).

A diverse crowd stands here in front of the 8th & H Street N.W. headquarters of the United States Christian Commission, including wounded soldiers, women, children, and free blacks. The Christian Commission was founded "to promote the spiritual and temporal welfare of the soldiers in the Army and the sailors in the Navy, in cooperation with the Chaplains." The commission later became the Y.M.C.A.

The 10th Veteran Reserve Corps was organized in New York City on October 10, 1863. Music played an important part in the Civil War. By the end of 1861, the Union Army had 618 bands and more than 28,000 musicians. The drum corps shown here includes a variety of instruments, including several string and wind instruments.

F Street just west of the Treasury in March 1865 with Hancock's Veteran Corps. Hancock's First Veteran Corps was not a regular army corps; rather it was the attempt to reenlist discharged veteran soldiers into U.S. rather than state units.

Company D of the 10th Veteran Reserve Corps poses in dress uniform, April 1865.

A group of men stand in front of the old War Department building near the time of Lincoln's assassination in April 1865.

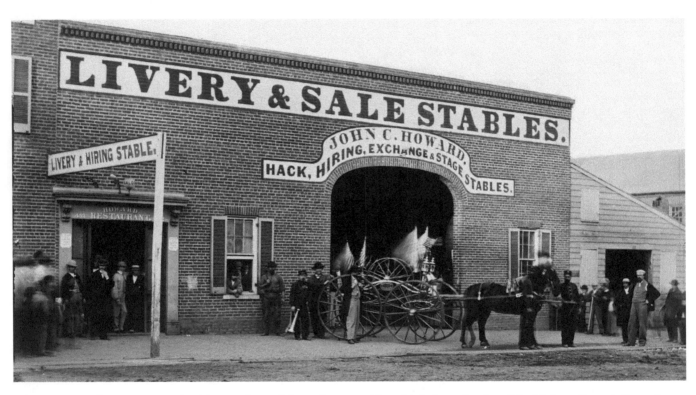

John C. Howard's restaurant and stables stands on G Street between 6th and 7th (now the site of the Verizon Center). It was here that John Wilkes Booth hired the horse on which he escaped after assassinating Lincoln.

A well-known view of the execution of the Lincoln assassination conspirators, showing them hanged at the Arsenal at Fort Humphries, on July 7, 1865. It was the first execution of a woman by the federal government.

Captain Henry Wirz, the commanding officer of the Confederate prisoner of war camp at Andersonville, is hanged in November 1865. For abuse of Union prisoners of war, after pleas for leniency that he was only following orders, Wirz became the only Confederate military officer tried, convicted, and hanged after the war.

The hooded body of Captain Wirz hanging from the scaffold, November 10, 1865. Within sight of the scaffold is the newly completed Capitol dome.

Ebbitt House, a residential hotel, here on the right, was a fixture in Washington social life. Its exuberant Second Empire mansard roof would be echoed a bit more sedately by the neighboring Willard Hotel. This image captures the bustle of F Street in 1880. Visible to the left is the tower on the (Baltimore) Sun building—then Washington's first skyscraper.

THE "NEW WASHINGTON" TO THE GILDED AGE
(1880–1920)

This photograph depicts the State, War, and Navy Building (now the Eisenhower Executive Office Building) near its completion in the late 1880s. The building, designed by then Supervising Architect of the Treasury Alfred B. Mullett, is of the French Second Empire style. At the time of its construction, the public looked upon the building with some disfavor, viewing it as too costly and stylistically pretentious. Mullett was denied his fee through contract dispute, the long struggle with the government prompting his 1890 suicide.

In a stunt that if performed today would immediately draw a swarm of Capitol police, Will Robertson of the Capital Bicycle Club rides down the steps of the Capitol in 1884.

Members of the Capital Bicycle Club line up for Herbert S. Owen's Birthday Run in 1888.

Although Washington is most usually shown in monuments and grand federal buildings, it also took pride in being a regular city, as shown in this 1889 view of 7th Street, N.W.

The Hay and Adams residences on the north of Lafayette Square were designed by the preeminent architect of his day, H. H. Richardson, in his distinctive Romanesque style. The two houses were for his friends John Hay (private secretary to Abraham Lincoln) and Henry Adams (writer, historian, and academic). Henry Adams would move into his house, but without his wife Marion, "Clover," who committed suicide in 1885 by drinking cyanide as the house was being finished. The houses were demolished in 1927 for the Hay-Adams Hotel.

Streetcars first appeared in Washington in 1860, then reached into the suburbs. Here is an Eckington and Soldiers' Home streetcar with experimental surface-contact equipment. This method of powering the streetcar ultimately failed, so parts of the line used battery power and even horses (ca. 1890).

In 1892 the Grand Army of the Republic Encampment returned to parade again in Washington, to the delight of tremendous crowds. But with the Twenty-sixth National Encampment, the G.A.R. began a long membership decline. The last member died in 1956 at the age of 109.

Major Russell B. Harrison, son of then-president Benjamin Harrison, poses with his children on the White House lawn sometime during his father's administration (1889–1893).

After the Civil War, the City of Washington began to expand, growing north toward Pacific (now Dupont) Circle. Substantial houses were built by wealthy newcomers to the area, as exemplified by this fine home at Connecticut Avenue and R Street, N.W. Designed by Hornblower and Marshall, it was built for George S. Fraser in 1890. It now houses the Church of Scientology.

Chief Justice Melville Fuller administers the oath of office to William McKinley in 1897. Former president Grover Cleveland stands to the right. McKinley's inauguration was the first to be captured by motion picture cameras and the first to be audio recorded.

This unusual image of turn-of-the-century Washington reverses the usual perspective, facing west on Pennsylvania Avenue toward the White House, rather than east toward the Capitol. The Washington Post building can be seen to the right, along with the new Willard Hotel, opened in 1904, and on the left the statue of Alexander Shepherd, erected in 1909.

The Grand Army of the Republic encampment still brought out huge crowds in October 1902, here crowding the steps and grounds of the Treasury at 15th Street and Pennsylvania Avenue. It had been ten years since the previous encampment in Washington.

Photographer Frances Benjamin Johnston here depicts an elegant carriage belonging to the Hearsts, at their Dupont Circle home, 1400 New Hampshire Avenue, N.W. Phoebe Apperson Hearst, wife of Senator George Hearst and mother of William Randolph Hearst, was herself very socially active, founding the National Cathedral School for Girls in Washington and what would become the national Parent Teacher Association (PTA).

A view southwest from the top of the Washington Monument, facing West Potomac Park and Hains Point. Reclamation of the Potomac flats began in 1882, and in 1897 the land was made parkland (ca. 1903).

A relatively rare view of Pennsylvania Avenue and downtown Washington from atop the Capitol. This turn-of-the-century image shows ordinary Washington—houses, churches, hotels, and offices—which surrounded the federal presence.

Suter's Tavern (ca. 1900), in Georgetown below the C&O Canal, at K and 31st streets, was a reminder of earliest Washington history. George Washington met the local area landowners there and persuaded them to sell land for the foundation of the new capital city.

A man sells strawberries on the streets of Washington in 1900 as two small boys look on.

Ford's Theater, site of the assassination of President Lincoln, served later as a federal office building. Originally a Baptist church, Ford leased it in 1861, and rebuilt it in 1863 after a fire. Closed as a theater immediately following the assassination, it also served as various military offices, including the Army Medical Museum for a time. In 1893 the collapse of three floors resulted in the death of 22 government clerks, and injuries to 68 more. After serving as a warehouse, the building was restored as a theater and reopened in 1968.

Ordinary business Washington as depicted in a turn-of-the-century survey photograph. This is E Street, N.W., facing east from 7th Street. Eiseman Bros. occupies the corner, now a Starbucks.

Church of the Covenant on Connecticut Avenue at N Street N.W. was nicknamed "Church of the Government" for all of the important officials who attended. The church later became National Presbyterian Church, which is now located on Nebraska Avenue, Tenleytown. Today an unimpressive office building fills this site, built after the landmark church was demolished in 1966.

A horse-drawn wagon makes a delivery to the White House in 1904.

The Stoneleigh Court Apartments were built by Secretary of State John Hay and his architect James G. Hill in 1902. The apartment building at Connecticut Avenue and L Street, among the largest and most luxurious in the city, was leveled in 1965.

Shepherd's Centennial Building was erected in the 1870s, at a time in Washington when the French-inspired Second Empire style was hugely popular. (The style was also called "General Grant's style" because of its wide use in federal buildings at the time.) The Centennial Building was converted into the Raleigh Hotel in the 1890s and then razed to make way for a new building in 1911.

F Street remained the main business thoroughfare of the city for many years, stretching from 7th Street to 15th Street, lined with shops and department stores. Most of the structures depicted here disappeared with downtown renewal efforts in the 1960s and 1970s.

This photograph depicts the new Willard Hotel shortly after its completion in 1901. The architect who designed the building, Henry Janeway Hardenbergh, also designed New York's Plaza Hotel. One of the city's first steel-framed buildings, the Willard was billed as Washington's first skyscraper.

A view of Pennsylvania Avenue from the Treasury (ca. 1904). To the left the new Willard Hotel has been completed. The south side has not yet been cleared for construction of the District Building. The Shepherd Centennial Building stands next to the Old Post Office.

President Taft and the First Lady ride back to the White House from the Capitol in a convertible. A technology enthusiast, Taft, elected in 1908, was the first president to use an automobile in an inauguration.

"The Boulevard" was a place for recreational driving in Potomac Park on reclaimed land from the Potomac River, here showing both horse-drawn carriages and automobiles. A 50-foot-wide macadam drive was first constructed along the east bank of the Tidal Basin. A riverside drive from the tidal basin inlet to 26th Street was funded in 1907, and in 1912 the first planting of cherry trees took place.

Inspired in part by Roman public bath complexes, Daniel Burnham, lead architect for the World's Columbian Exposition in Chicago, designed Washington's Union Station. This picture captures that building before the statuary of Louis Saint-Gaudens was placed on the entablature over the triple-arched entrance and before the addition of the Columbus Fountain (ca. 1910).

A trolley car runs from the Capitol toward Lincoln Park and the Eastern Car House (now the Car Barn condominiums) on Capitol Hill.

Famed photographer Lewis Hine captures a group of "dime messenger" boys for the National Child Labor Committee. For seven dollars a week young boys delivered telegrams throughout the city. Progressive-era reformers objected to this kind of child labor, and through his photography, Hine was instrumental in ending it.

A view of Luther Place Memorial Church and the statue of Martin Luther (ca. 1905). Constructed in 1874, the church burnt in 1904 and was reopened and rededicated by President Roosevelt in 1905. Officially known as Memorial Evangelical Lutheran Church, the church takes its unofficial name from the statue of Martin Luther erected in 1884.

Taft Bridge on Connecticut Avenue, soon after opening in 1907. Begun in 1897, the cost and lengthy construction earned this bridge the nickname "the Million Dollar Bridge." It was named for President Taft in 1931. Replacing a low iron-truss bridge from 1888, Taft Bridge was built of unreinforced concrete to a bold and widely admired design by George Morrison and Edward Casey.

Photographer Lewis Hine captures a group of young "newsies" selling papers on the steps of the Capitol in 1912. The youngest is eight years old.

Washington's largest independent drugstore chain was Peoples Drug Store. This particular store was the site of extended picketing by African Americans in the 1930s because the chain refused to hire blacks.

White House photographers eat on the White House lawn in the 1920s. President Warren Harding opened the first pressroom for photographers in 1921, shortly after the creation of the White House News Photographers Association.

This image depicts the new Woodward & Lothrop building at 1003 F Street, N.W., in 1912. In subsequent years, the department store would continue to build in the block flanked by 11th and F streets and 10th and G streets, ultimately entirely filling it (with the sole exception of Rich's Shoes).

Photographer Herbert E. French records Woodrow Wilson returning to the White House in 1913, with his naval and military aides.

On a snowy day in Washington, D.C., a policeman drinks coffee while a driver and his passenger look on (ca. 1910).

Photographed by Lewis Hine in front of the Washington Post building, this young man worked well into the night delivering telegrams for Western Union.

A busy day for streetcars, automobiles, vendor carts, and pedestrians is in progress around 1912, in the eastern area of downtown, at F Street between 6th and 7th streets. The north side of this street is occupied today by the Verizon Center.

Lewis Hine depicts a young messenger boy in the foreground standing in Washington's notorious red-light district at C and 13th streets, N.W. The boy told Hine he delivered messages there until 10 P.M.

Washington's streetcar system was extremely popular. Here pedestrians rush to board and debark streetcars at a transfer spot at 15th Street and New York Avenue east of the Treasury and White House (ca. 1920).

Security for the President has always been a concern, as guards and bollards are evidence of here. The ornate White House gates, shown here during the Wilson administration around 1913, were replaced with sturdier ones modeled on the originals. The 900-pound originals were removed and repaired. Restored to their original green color, they have been placed on exhibit at the American Horticultural Society.

A view of the 600 block (632 and 634), south side of Pennsylvania Avenue, N.W., ca. 1926. Just west of Washington's original Chinatown, these storefronts would soon be demolished to make way for a portion of the Federal Triangle.

A group of debutantes walk under the Tidal Basin cherry blossoms in the early 1920s. The flowering cherry trees were a gift from the Japanese government. The first ones sent over in 1910, infected with insects and plant diseases, had to be burned. The replacements proved suitable and have been a very popular part of every visitor's Washington.

Employees of the Washington Battery Company pose in front of their storefront at 1623 L Street, N.W., in 1919. Automobile dealers clustered along nearby blocks of 14th Street.

The Patent Office Building, at left, from the corner of G and 9th streets, N.W., ca. 1920.

The Herman Building was designed for Abraham Herman in the 1890s by local architects Paul Schulze and Albert Goenner. The building still stands at 7th and H streets, N.W., as part of the renewed commercial strip.

General Pershing congratulates one of the Alaskan Flyers in 1920. U.S. Army Air Service fliers flew four modified World War I DH-4B bombers from New York to Nome, Alaska, and back. The entire trip covered 9,000 miles. The flight began July 15, 1920, and arrived at Nome, Alaska, on August 24. The same planes and crews returned on October 20.

Outside Smith Transfer and Storage at 13th and U streets, N.W., ca. 1920, the company moving fleet is mobilized for action. Denizens of today's U Street, surrounded by new apartments, condominiums, restaurants, and nightclubs, would find this leafy and sedate view quite unfamiliar.

Peoples Drug Store was Washington's largest independent drugstore chain. In the 1930s, the NAACP protested Peoples' practice of serving food to black customers on paper plates while serving whites with china.

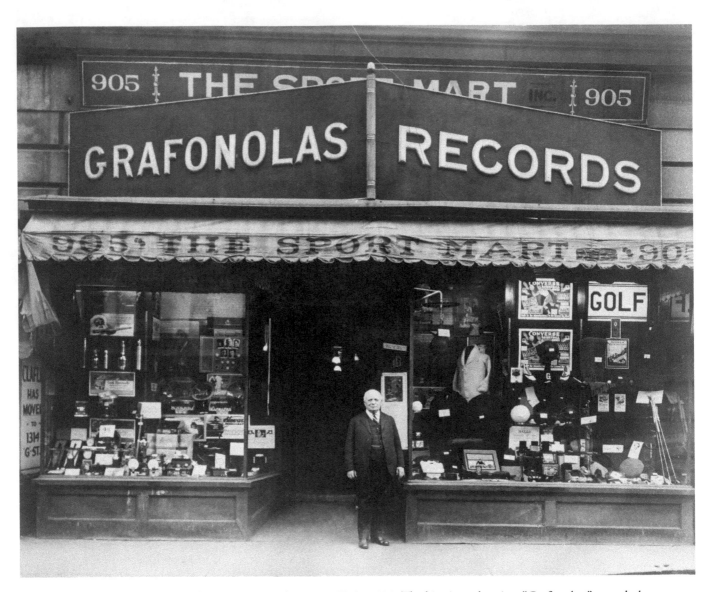

This is a picture of a sporting goods store at 905 F Street, N.W., in 1920. The big sign advertises "Grafonolas," record players made by the Columbia Corporation.

Sculptor Daniel Chester French's *Rear Admiral Samuel Francis DuPont Memorial Fountain* is dedicated in 1921. DuPont was the first naval hero of the Civil War. The three figures on the fountain represent the Sea, the Stars, and the Wind.

Santa rides the back of an extravagantly decorated truck, appealing on behalf of the U.S. postal service for early mailing (December 10, 1921).

Isolationism to War

(1921–1949)

The Peoples Drug Store on the southeastern corner of 7th Street and Massachusetts Avenue, N.W., is exuberantly covered with ads in 1921.

A group of World War I veterans meet at the White House in 1921 with President Warren Harding to appeal for the release of some federal prisoners.

The Leader Theater was one of many first-run movie houses on 9th Street. Its architecture was especially fantastical, with classical figures adorning its facade. In this view, Jackie Coogan gets top billing over Charlie Chaplin in *The Kid*.

Famed magician and escape artist Harry Houdini is suspended here in 1922 from atop B. F. Keith's Theater. He draws a crowd to witness his upside-down straitjacket escape.

Manager Clyde Milan of the Washington Nationals and Miller Huggins of the Yankees shake hands before the game, April 12, 1922. President Harding threw out the first ball. Babe Ruth was out of the Yankee lineup, suspended by the league, so he watched the game from the presidential box. The Nats out-hit the Yankees 15-9, and beat them 6-5, coming from behind to win in the 8th.

In 1922, a fire destroyed the ballroom of the Willard Hotel. Among the guests who were roused from their beds that night were Calvin Coolidge and John Philip Sousa.

Babe Ruth acknowledges his fans during his last "at bat" at Griffith Stadium (September 30, 1924).

Crowds line the route along Pennsylvania Avenue as members of the pennant-winning Nationals baseball team make their way to meet the President, October 1, 1924.

"Tige," the White House cat, returns home after his disappearance is announced on Washington radio (March 25, 1924). President Coolidge observed, "Any man who does not like dogs and want them about does not deserve to be in the White House," but the Coolidges were also very attached to their pet cats, birds, wombats, and raccoons.

During the 1920s, electric traffic signals were introduced to the streets of Washington. This one stood at the intersection of New Hampshire and 18th streets, N.W.

Crowds stand outside First Congregational Church on April 12, 1925, where President Coolidge and the First Lady are attending Easter services. According to *Time* magazine, "On Easter Sunday, the President and Mrs. Coolidge attended divine service at the First Congregational Church, to which Mr. Coolidge had sent White House flowers. Their clothes were smart, not new." This Gothic church no longer stands, replaced in 1961 by an inconspicuous modern structure, demolished in the late 2000s.

Baseball fans crowd 11th Street in 1925 to watch the World Series scoreboard posted on the Evening Star building. They would be disappointed. After winning the pennant in 1924, Washington blew a 3-1 lead to lose the World Series.

U.S. Army blimps, the T.C. 5 and T.C. 9, from Langley Field, pass over the Washington Monument during a practice flight in the 1920s.

During Prohibition, federal agents would halt motorists to search for illicit alcohol. Novelty shops sold signs like the one shown here.

A Washington Rapid Transit Co. bus appears at the intersection of 13th and F streets, N.W. (ca. 1925).

Arlington Memorial Bridge is under construction sometime around 1929. Like the Lincoln Memorial itself, Arlington Bridge was seen as a symbolic rejoining of North and South, connecting the Lincoln Memorial and Arlington Cemetery. The bridge opened with no celebration on January 16, 1932.

Arlington Memorial Bridge, as seen from the south bank on the Virginia shore. The bridge took six years to build and was a monumental extension of the McMillan Commission plan for the Mall across the Potomac to Arlington Cemetery.

An aerial view of Arlington Memorial Bridge. Visible in this image is the central draw span—once one of the longest, heaviest, and fastest, it is now sealed shut (ca. 1931).

Harry Wardman, leading Washington developer, erected the Shoreham Building at the corner of 15th and H streets, N.W., in 1928, replacing the Shoreham Hotel. Newspapers at the time identified the building's style as "modernized Greek."

Newly inaugurated President Herbert Hoover greets enthusiastic citizens at the White House on March 4, 1929. Well-wishers crowded the White House grounds following the inauguration. His words "I have no fears for the future of our country. It is bright with hope" were to be challenged with the coming of the Great Depression.

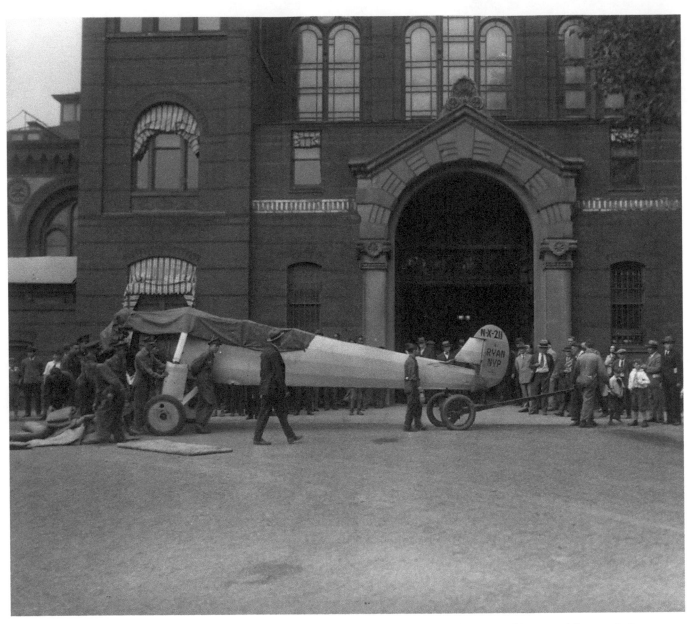

In May 1928, the Smithsonian received one of its most important and popular items: the *Spirit of St. Louis*. The year before, Charles Lindbergh had flown the plane around the country in a 92-city promotional tour. Millions of Americans saw the plane either on the ground or flying over their city.

Joining the new president at the White House was his Belgian police dog, King Tut, shown here with officer W. S. Newton on April 11, 1929. Even if the Coolidge menagerie could not be outdone, a photograph of the presidential dog was always newsworthy.

This 1928 view of
Pennsylvania Avenue
facing the Capitol from
the Treasury steps shows
a scene now filled with
automobiles, as well as
the venerable streetcars.
In the lower-right corner
is a traffic policeman at
his station, shaded from
the sun by an umbrella.

A view of a rather barren Pennsylvania Avenue, from 4th Street toward the Capitol. Missouri Avenue had been closed and the buildings lining it razed, for expansion of the Mall, leaving the south side of Pennsylvania Avenue empty. The north side was being readied for a District government "Municipal Center" to rival the Federal Triangle. Evidence of construction of the Supreme Court Building is visible in the distance (ca. 1930).

A crowd of military band members and a small boy wait on N Street, S.W., in this Louise Rosskam slice of life portrait. All are participating in an unusually public wedding ceremony at Barney Neighborhood House (the Duncanson-Cranch House) ca. 1938.

A Park Police officer feeds pigeons in Lafayette Square in front of the statue of Andrew Jackson around 1930. Lafayette Square remains to this day a popular green space for relaxation and recreation.

The Westory Building, once called the "Flatiron Building's rival" because of its narrowness, was built by developer George H. Higbee in 1907. Higbee paid $76 a square foot to acquire the land at F and 14th streets, N.W., at the time the highest price paid for real estate in Washington.

The Federal Trade Commission Building, designed by architect Edward H. Bennett, sits at the apex of the Federal Triangle grouping of public buildings. This photograph was made near the time of its completion in 1938. The building's lack of ornamentation and detail reflects a somber, Depression-era spirit. Federal Triangle represents one of the nation's last executed plans of the City Beautiful movement.

A view of the Jefferson Memorial, nearly two years before its official dedication in April 1943, held to coincide with the 200th anniversary of Thomas Jefferson's birth. John Russell Pope designed the memorial and the National Gallery of Art, under construction across the Mall at the same time. As the popularity of the modern movement in architecture grew, many critics saw the memorial as out of step with the times because of its reliance on classical forms.

Photographer Martha Roberts snapped this picture of soldiers and civilians at a shooting gallery on a Saturday afternoon on 9th Street, N.W., in July 1941.

Even World War II didn't interrupt the traditional White House Easter egg roll in 1944, here depicted in a Farm Security Administration photograph, part of the Portrait of America series.

On November 28, 1944, a B-29 Super Fortress is on display at Washington National Airport. Journalists lined up to see the new plane, which had recently bombed Japan.

A nation mourns the death of Franklin Roosevelt, whose funeral procession moves along the streets of Washington on April 14, 1945.

Harry Truman is inaugurated, January 20, 1949. A throng gathers at the East Front of the Capitol to observe the new president take the oath of office.

Noted sculptor Daniel Chester French sculptured the statue of Lincoln in the Lincoln Memorial. The memorial, one of Washington's most popular, was dedicated in 1922. This inspired image was recorded in 1951.

Postwar Growth and Decline

(1950–1963)

Bruce Wahl's beer garden, on 4th Street between C and Maryland Avenue, S.W., was a very popular nightspot in 1954. In its earlier incarnation as Mike's, the place had featured crabcakes and beer; it was Wahl who added live entertainment.

A woman waits for a bus on M Street, S.W., in 1958. The tower of the St. Vincent de Paul church is visible in the background. The buildings behind her are unusual stone-faced houses, designed by noted and prolific Washington architect Appleton P. Clark, Jr., for the Washington Sanitary Housing Company, in 1907. Washington Sanitary Housing Company built high-quality housing in depressed areas of the city and was the original private urban renewal effort in Southwest Washington—half a century before federal urban renewal. This row of houses no longer exists.

This image shows the crowd on the Mall during the 1963 March on Washington.

A view from the Lincoln Memorial on August 28, 1963, the day Martin Luther King, Jr., delivered his "I Have a Dream" speech.

Attorney General Robert F. Kennedy speaks to a crowd outside the Justice Department in June 1963. A man holds a sign reading "Congress of Racial Equality" (CORE), a civil rights organization that was one of the sponsors of the March on Washington for Jobs and Freedom later that summer.

Marchers carry signs for equal rights, integrated schools, better housing, and an end to bias, during the 1963 "March on Washington for Jobs and Freedom."

Notes on the Photographs

These notes, listed by page number, attempt to include all aspects known of the photographs. Each of the photographs is identified by the page number, a title or description, photographer and collection, archive, and call or box number when applicable. Although every attempt was made to collect all data, in some cases complete data may have been unavailable due to the age and condition of some of the photographs and records.

Printed in the USA
CPSIA information can be obtained
at www.ICGtesting.com
JSHW072022140824
68134JS00042B/3750